21st Century Skills INNOVATION Library

Cars

by James M. Flammang

Published in the United States of America by Cherry Lake Publishing
Ann Arbor, Michigan
www.cherrylakepublishing.com

Content Adviser: Amy C. Newman, Director, Forney Museum of Transportation

Design: The Design Lab

Photo Credits: Cover and page 3, ©Oleksiy Maksymenko/Alamy; page 4, ©Transtock Inc./Alamy;
page 6, ©Christophe Testi/Alamy; page 8, ©North Wind Picture Archives/Alamy; page 11, ©Roger
Dale Pleis, used under license from Shutterstock, Inc.; page 12, ©iStockphoto.com/travelif; page
15, ©ClassicStock/Alamy; pages 16 and 26, ©The Print Collector/Alamy; page 19, ©Kathy
deWitt/Alamy; page 20, ©iStockphoto.com/MCCAIG; page 22, ©ARCTIC IMAGES/Alamy; page 23,
©iStockphoto.com/binabina; page 25, ©AP Photo/HO; page 28, ©Mary Evans Picture Library/
Alamy; page 29, ©Stan Rohrer/Alamy

Library of Congress Cataloging-in-Publication Data
Flammang, James M.
 Cars / by James M. Flammang.
   p. cm.–(Innovation in transportation)
 Includes bibliographical references and index.
 ISBN-13: 978-1-60279-231-9
 ISBN-10: 1-60279-231-3
 1. Automobiles–History–Juvenile literature. 2. Automobile industry and
trade–United States–History–Juvenile literature. I. Title. II. Series.
 TL147.F55412 2009
 629.222–dc22   2008002047

*Cherry Lake Publishing would like to acknowledge the work of
The Partnership for 21st Century Skills.
Please visit www.21stcenturyskills.org for more information.*

CONTENTS

INNOVATION IN TRANSPORTATION

CHAPTER ONE

Getting Behind the Wheel

Stock cars are automobiles that have specially designed engines and bodies that help them go very fast.

The crowd cheers wildly as two race cars speed around a turn. The incredible machines fly by in a blur. To go this fast—200 miles (322 kilometers) per hour—NASCAR racers require a lot of high-tech equipment.

Years ago, no one imagined that one day it would be possible to build an automobile that could move at those speeds. These machines didn't develop overnight. It took years of work by many inventors, trained engineers, and designers to make cars the high-performance machines they are today.

Karl Benz and Gottlieb Daimler created the first automobiles in Europe in the 1880s. In 1896, Charles Duryea was the first American to start an automobile company. Duryea built only 13 cars before giving up the automotive business. People were not buying the cars. They couldn't afford them, and they didn't see a practical use for them. But that was about to change.

By 1900, there were about 8,000 cars on the road in the United States. More people began to see the convenience of the automobile. It gave them the freedom to travel farther and faster. The days of horse-drawn buggies were slowly coming to an end.

Most early cars were noisy, smelly, and difficult to drive. They were also expensive. Rural people often feared automobiles, claiming that they would "scare the horses." Roads were little more than rutted paths for horses and wagons. Even a short trip in a car could be difficult with these harsh road conditions. Detroit got the country's first mile of concrete highway in 1908. Gradually, dirt roads were improved with smoother **asphalt**. This "paved" the way for more American automotive innovators to release their newest cars.

By the 1920s, half of the vehicles in the world were Model Ts.

Henry Ford is probably the most famous of all American automobile innovators. When his Model T Ford was launched in 1908, no one imagined the mobility it would provide to millions of families. Ford said he wanted the car to be "so low in price that no man making a good salary will be unable to own one."

People loved the Model T for its simple design. It was both tough and durable. Many owners could also do their own repairs, which made car maintenance easier. The Ford Model T completely revolutionized the industry. It set the standard for American-made cars for years to come.

Since the early days of the automotive industry, there have been many innovations from different car manufacturers. But the industry has not been without its challenges. It has suffered through labor strikes, world wars, oil crises, and struggling economies. Despite these setbacks, the industry has also seen its share of success stories. These include muscle cars, minivans, safety innovations, and even hydrogen-fueled automobiles. Today, the automotive industry continues to create new and exciting products that keep people moving.

Learning & Innovation Skills

Until the 1960s, Americans didn't think much about the impact of automobiles on the environment. Even today, many place their desire for a big car ahead of environmental issues. Growing levels of smog prompted laws that forced auto companies to make engines that produce fewer pollutants. But people concerned about the environment say those laws aren't strict enough.

Why do you think so many people choose to ignore the environment and purchase big cars that use more gas and create more pollution? What do you think should be done about this?

CHAPTER TWO

Innovations in Technology and Equipment

NEW MODEL
NUMBER SIX

BABCOCK ELECTRIC VICTORIA PHAETON

*Easy to Operate—Easy to get into—Easy to ride in—Easy
to keep clean in—Easy to get out of—Easy to maintain*

PRICE COMPLETE, $1,600.00. All Necessary Equipment Include

No expense has been spared to bring this new No. 6 car up to the very highest standard of carriage making.
While it is built along the lines of the most approved types, it possesses an added grace, luxurious style, and fine fini
at give it a distinguished appearance not found in any other car on the market.
Owing to its high speed and long mileage, it is well adapted to both business and pleasure.
This carriage will show a speed of twenty-six miles an hour for short spurts. The regular running speed is from thirte
eighteen miles per hour, and when properly operated, over good level, macadam roads, it will travel from seventy-fi
eighty-five miles on one charge of the batteries. A mechanical duplicate of this car recently made a run from Ne
ork to Philadelphia (100 miles) without recharging the batteries.

OTHER DESIRABLE FEATURES

The body is of the "Victoria" type, with full "Victoria" top, equipped with continuous leather fenders.
It is upholstered in either blue or green broadcloth, the body being painted to match.
TIRES. 32 x 3 inches. Special Clincher No. 410. WHEELS. 32 inches front and back.
DRIVING GEAR. (Double chain) is so constructed as to be very flexible and noiseless (no shirring). and starts smoothl
BRAKES. Powerful expanding brakes in hub of both rear wheels and auxiliary brake on motor counter-shaft.
RANGE OF SPEED. 6 to 26 miles per hour. WEIGHT. About 1,600 pounds.
MOTOR AND CONTROLLER. 1½ H.P. (normal), with 300 per cent. overload capacity. Is suspended from chas
der seat. Our own design, with four forward speeds, and the gears run in addition to which, there is an accelerat

erits of this or
ectric Carriag
you will alwe
FALO

The first electric cars lost favor with consumers
because they cost a lot of money to operate.

As automobile popularity
grew, hundreds of companies
jumped into car manufacturing.
Many were satisfied to
copy the efforts of others.
Some inventors had ideas
of their own. Step by step,
the automobile evolved in
performance and comfort.

In the late 1890s, three
propulsion systems competed
for dominance: steam, electric,
and gasoline. The Stanley
Steamer was the best-known
steam-powered automobile.

It was produced until 1927. Steam-powered vehicles needed fuel to heat the water to the boiling point. Once the water was boiling, the steam it produced powered the engine. The drawback with steam-powered engines was that they took awhile to get started in the morning. For the average automobile driver, it took too long to heat up the water. Steam-powered automobiles fell out of favor as the Ford Model T took over more of the market. People preferred the Model T because it ran on gasoline and was easier to start.

Early in the 20th century, electric cars were the most popular cars for a time. Electric-powered automobiles used no fuel, which was an advantage. Batteries provided all of the power. Electric cars were also quiet. Women, in particular, liked the quiet behavior of models such as the Baker Electric and Detroit Electric. Doctors also preferred the electric cars, which started up consistently. But the automobile's batteries didn't last long before they had to be recharged. Many people were stranded on the roads with no power to run their cars. As a result, the electric-powered automobile also lost popularity. Many people switched to the more reliable gasoline-fueled car.

Despite their noise and odors, gasoline engines promised greater power and reliability than steam or electric systems. At the time, oil that could be refined into gasoline was plentiful. Ford's popular Model T used gasoline. Gas engines became the standard propulsion system used by American automobile manufacturers for much of the 20th century.

Gasoline engines can be large or small. They can have a single **cylinder** or several cylinders. The motor can be in the front of the car, in the rear, or under the seat. To get up to speed, the car needed a **transmission** with **gears**. A transmission allows the driver to shift from one gear to the next as the engine speed increases. The gears make the engine's power more efficient while increasing the speed of the car.

Early cars used levers to shift gears while driving. Many people had difficulty physically switching gears with the lever. Ford, with his combination of technical knowledge and desire to sell autos, addressed this problem. The Model T used a simpler design, known as the **planetary** transmission. The driver changed gears not by moving a shift lever, but by pushing floor-mounted pedals. This made it easier to switch gears.

The next innovation in this area was the automatic transmission. As early as 1904, a transmission that shifted gears by itself was being installed on automobiles. Many people today still prefer cars that have an automatic transmission.

Early automobiles were difficult to drive. Operating them required physical strength. Drivers used iron hand

A man died in 1910 after an accident involving a hand crank. Creative thinkers worked hard to come up with safer ways to start automobiles.

cranks to start them. Without perfect timing and some luck, an engine could backfire and the crank could injure a person. Inventor Charles Kettering worked to solve that problem. His **electric starter** was installed on 1912 Cadillacs. By the 1920s, nearly every new car had one. Sales, especially to women, went up because the hand crank was no longer needed to start the car.

Brakes in the early days operated on only two wheels. Brakes work by pressing down on a foot pedal to slow the car to a stop. In the early days, one needed considerable leg strength to physically stop the car with the pedal. Auto designers and engineers developed the hydraulic brakes we use today to make braking easier. Hydraulic brakes require less effort. They provide more effective braking with just a push of your leg.

It is easy to overlook the importance of windshield wipers. Before they were invented, it was much harder to drive in bad weather.

Early car designs looked more like horse-drawn buggies without the horses. They were big, awkward, clunky-looking machines. After World War II, auto designers created cars with a sleeker, more modern appearance. Engineers worked with designers to create cars that were more aerodynamic and able to achieve higher speeds.

Innovators didn't stop thinking about engines after gasoline power became the standard. They kept tinkering with engines to make them better. Eventually, powerful V-8 engines pushed aside earlier designs. A "horsepower race" took place during the 1950s and 1960s. Engine power is measured in terms of horsepower. Auto companies started competing to see who could make the most powerful engine.

During this same period, power-operated accessories grew popular. Auto companies worked to make cars more comfortable and easier to operate. They knew that new features were needed to attract new buyers or get people to upgrade to newer models. Soon cars were equipped with power door locks, windows, mirrors, and seats. Air-conditioning and radios became standard in most cars. Power-assisted brakes and steering made driving less tiring.

Through most of the 20th century, fuel prices in the United States were low compared to those in the

Learning & Innovation Skills

Many safety features were first installed on expensive automobiles only. Eventually, these features were added to economical cars as well. Some General Motors cars had air bags in the 1970s, but most people never knew they existed. Since the 1980s, the U.S. government has required front air bags. Inventors worked on seat-mounted air bags and curtain-type air bags. Both types provide a cushion to help protect passengers in the event of a collision.

Antilock brakes help prevent a car's wheels from skidding on slippery pavement. They were first installed on Mercedes-Benz models. Electronic Stability Control, which helps the driver control a vehicle, first appeared in 1997. These innovations have made cars safer to drive.

Why do you think most safety innovations first appeared on expensive cars?

rest of the world. As prices rise, however, there is renewed interest in fuel economy. Some people look for smaller, more fuel-efficient cars. Others have turned to the new "green" **hybrids**, which run on a combination of gasoline and electric (battery) power. Hybrids consume less fuel and emit fewer pollutants. Once again, auto innovators are turning their attention to creating solutions to the fuel economy problem. Manufacturers know that they need to respond to the demands of consumers if they want to sell their cars.

CHAPTER THREE

Selling Cars

Auto companies can't just make cars. They also have to convince people to buy them. Some creative thinkers came up with the idea of holding auto shows. Few people in the early 1900s knew how to drive an automobile. In fact, many people had rarely or never seen an automobile. Auto companies began setting up test-drive tracks at auto shows. They wanted to help people learn how to drive. They reasoned that this was one way to get more drivers behind the wheel.

Manufacturers realized that one effective way of selling automobiles was to have polite salespeople present cars in attractive showrooms.

Henry Ford knew that it would take more than just teaching people how to drive to sell more cars. He knew that for most people to be able to buy cars, they had to be less expensive. In the early days, cars were assembled by hand. Because they took more hours of labor to make, they were more expensive.

Ford figured out how to use mass production to make that possible. His moving **assembly line** went into operation in 1913. Workers would stay in one place. The cars would come to them by moving from one work station to the next. Assembly line workers needed

Ford's original mass production plant was located in Highland Park, Michigan.

fewer skills. They didn't have to know how to put together the entire car. Also, because they were doing the same task over and over, they learned to complete their tasks more quickly. Soon other manufacturers adopted the assembly line method of manufacturing autos. It is still the method by which most autos are made.

Keeping a car for many years doesn't keep the industry successful. Even in the early 20th century, manufacturers constantly worked to come up with ideas to encourage drivers to buy new ones. Late in the 1920s, Alfred P. Sloan, president of General Motors, adopted annual styling changes for each model. His idea became known as "planned obsolescence." When a new car model came out, new ads were created. Manufacturers used the ads to try to make owners believe that their old cars weren't good enough anymore.

21st Century Content

Today, many of the "workers" who assemble automobiles get no wages, take no breaks, and never complain. That's because they're robots, performing their tasks automatically. Companies now use robots to piece together car parts. This reduces the cost of manufacturing. Many people are upset about the use of robots in the industry, because they take jobs away from human workers.

CHAPTER FOUR

Automobiles in the Future

Cars of the early 21st century don't look at all like the automobiles of a century ago. New and exciting innovations are changing the way cars are made.

After World War II, people came up with creative ideas for future cars. Some suggested that one day everyone would be flying their own cars. Others said that cars would run on nuclear power. Some people even believed that someday cars might drive themselves, while occupants gazed at the scenery. But not all ideas end up as successful products.

Nuclear-powered automobiles never happened. Over the years, several inventors built flying cars, but few have been sold. In the 1990s, Buick demonstrated a car that drove without human attention on a stretch of "intelligent" highway. Sensors built into the pavement

Smart cars are popular in Europe. Do you think these small, fuel-efficient cars will catch on around the world?

guided the vehicle. Few people in the auto industry believe that a driverless automobile will attract customers.

Alternative power sources are still being developed. For many years, critics of the auto industry have called for smaller, more fuel-efficient cars. The federal government enacted fuel-economy standards in the 1970s. But average gas mileage has fallen far short of expectations. Late in 2007, the U.S. Congress passed a bill requiring that new cars get an average of 35 miles per gallon (mpg) (56 km per gallon) by the year 2020.

By 2008, most car manufacturers were offering hybrid automobiles as a choice for consumers.

If people are working on alternatives to gas-guzzling cars, why are we still so dependent on oil? The answer is because no one has come up with a car that runs on alternative fuel and is attractive to a large number of consumers.

Dozens, if not hundreds, of inventors have built electric cars. During the 1970s, quite a few small cars powered by electric motors were sold. But battery life remains an obstacle. Today's batteries are better but still can't provide sufficient range for most drivers' needs. Most electric cars can only be driven 50 to 100 miles (81 to 161 km) before they need to be plugged in for recharging. One recent exception is the Tesla sports car. The Tesla performs better than most regular sports cars and goes farther on a charge than other electrics. So what's the problem that still needs to be solved? The Tesla isn't exactly affordable for most consumers. The 2008 Tesla Roadster sells for a whopping $98,000!

Hybrid automobiles were developed as a compromise between gasoline and battery power. Part of the time, hybrid cars operate on batteries that feed energy to electric motors that drive the wheels. When necessary, the gasoline engine provides additional power. To save fuel, some car models have the gas engine shut off when the car comes to a stop.

Fuel-cell vehicles, with hydrogen as a fuel source, have been promised since the 1990s. A few hydrogen-

Time will tell if hydrogen will become the fuel of the future. Companies are working to make improved, more affordable hydrogen-powered cars.

powered cars are in use, such as Honda's FCX. Yet most experts believe they won't be practical until 2015 or 2020. There has to be a network of hydrogen refueling stations before people begin buying this car and others like it.

Designers and engineers are sure to continue working on the fuel problem. They also continue to come up with new safety and convenience features. Navigation systems are one recent addition to the list of car options. The systems help drivers find where they need to go. They rely on satellites in orbit around the earth that make up the Global Positioning System (GPS). First introduced in the 1990s, these navigation systems display a map on a screen and give route directions.

A GPS system is an attractive feature for many auto buyers.

Learning & Innovation Skills

One way to cut down on fuel usage is to take a bus or train. People can commute to work on bicycles, too. Buses and trains consume a lot of fuel, but carry large numbers of people. Car-sharing programs have sprung up for people who need an automobile only occasionally. Getting around American suburbs without a motor vehicle can be difficult. But many city residents could manage without one. Would you be willing to take mass transit to school or work, rather than travel in a car? Why or why not?

Backup warnings and rear-view cameras, which inform the driver of obstacles, are also likely to become more common. Lane Departure Warning systems, which signal when a vehicle strays from its course, may become standard. More exciting innovations are sure to make cars better and safer as we drive through the 21st century.

CHAPTER FIVE

Some Famous Innovators

Many individuals contributed to the development of automobiles and the automotive industry. Here are a few of the best-known innovators.

Karl Benz

Karl Benz is credited with developing the first real gasoline-powered automobile. Trained as a mechanical engineer, Benz became a draftsman and

Karl Benz (right) makes a test run with his gas-powered automobile.

Life & Career Skills

Early innovators tended to work alone. Henry Ford, Ransom Olds, and other automobile pioneers relied largely on their own efforts. Not as many individuals stand out in recent years. Instead, technical development has become a group process. Teams of engineers, scientists, designers, and others work together to reach a goal. Part of each workday may be spent in a workshop or laboratory. But they get together regularly to discuss their progress and see how their work fits with that of their colleagues.

designer. In 1868, he went to work for a bridge construction firm. In 1871, he founded his own machinery company. Three versions of his three-wheeled motor vehicle were designed in 1885–1887. He was granted a **patent** in 1886 and called his vehicle the Benz Patent Motor Car.

Gottlieb Daimler

Before studying mechanical engineering, Gottlieb Daimler **apprenticed** as a gunsmith. He later became a manager at a company where Nikolaus Otto was developing the four-stroke gasoline engine. In his home workshop, Daimler experimented with gasoline engines based on Otto's principles. He and Wilhelm Maybach first installed an engine in a motorcycle. Daimler was awarded a patent in 1885. His "motorized carriage" was the world's first four-wheeled motorcar. Eventually, the Benz and Daimler companies merged into what became Mercedes-Benz.

Daimler took what he learned from Otto and expanded on it to create his own gas engine.

Henry Ford

Born in Michigan, Henry Ford loved to tinker with different inventions. On June 4, 1896, he finished a four-wheeled vehicle. In 1903, with a group of investors, he formed the Ford Motor Company. Ford produced a series of car models in the early part of the century. The Model T, introduced in October 1908, brought motoring to the public. Because of the Model T's popularity, many Americans believe that Henry Ford invented the automobile.

Ford was the first manufacturer to pay his workers $5 for an 8-hour workday. Those were good wages at the time.

CREATIVITY

PERSEVERANCE

CURIOSITY

CHARLES F. KETTERING

Great innovators know how to overcome challenges. Kettering struggled with poor eyesight, but he went on to make important contributions in the automotive industry.

Charles F. Kettering

Best known for his electric starter, Charles Kettering was a creative inventor. After earning an engineering degree, he went on to become a co-founder of DELCO (Dayton Engineering Laboratories Company). While at DELCO, he contributed to many automotive innovations. Nicknamed "Boss Ket," he was named vice president of General Motors Research Corporation after DELCO and General Motors merged in 1920.

Glossary

apprenticed (uh-PREN-tisst) learned a trade by working with someone skilled for a specified period of time

asphalt (ASS-fawlt) a common material used to pave roads and highways

assembly line (uh-SEM-blee LINE) a series of work stations in a factory where the product moves from one worker to the next

brakes (BRAYKS) mechanical or hydraulic systems that cause a vehicle to stop when a pedal is pushed

cylinder (SIL-uhn-dur) part of an engine that is shaped like a tube

electric starter (i-LEK-trik START-ur) an electric motor used to crank a gasoline engine so it will begin running

gears (GIHRZ) small wheels with teeth that join with other gears inside a transmission

hybrids (HYE-bridz) vehicles that run on a combination of battery (electric) power and gasoline

patent (PAT-uhnt) a legal document giving an inventor the sole rights to manufacture and sell his or her invention

planetary (PLAN-uh-tair-ee) a type of transmission used in Ford's Model T

propulsion (pruh-PUHL-shuhn) the act of propelling, or moving something forward

transmission (trans-MISH-uhn) set of gears that delivers engine power to the wheels

For More Information

BOOKS

Collier, James Lincoln. *The Automobile*. Tarrytown, NY: Marshall Cavendish Benchmark, 2006.

Conley, Robyn. *The Automobile*. New York: Franklin Watts, 2005.

Corbett, David. *A History of Cars*. Milwaukee, WI: Gareth Stevens Publishing, 2006.

Cunningham, David. *The History of the Automobile*. Chanhassen, MN: The Child's World, 2005.

WEB SITES

The Museum of Automobile History
www.themuseumofautomobilehistory.com
See what's new at the Syracuse, New York, museum

Who Invented the Automobile? Everyday Mysteries: Fun Science Facts from the Library of Congress
www.loc.gov/rr/scitech/mysteries/auto.html
Read about fascinating automobile firsts and famous innovators

Index

About the Author

James M. Flammang is a journalist and author, who specializes in automobiles and transportation topics. Technology is one of his primary interests. In addition to evaluating and reviewing new cars and trucks, and writing buying advice for consumers, he has written more than 20 books about the history of the automobile. Since 1995, he has written about cars on his Web site, www.tirekick.com. In addition to titles in the Innovation in Transportation series, he has written three other books for young readers. He lives in Elk Grove Village, Illinois, and travels extensively to drive the latest car models.